FOUNDATIONAL TRUTHS

❖ Foundations of the Faith ❖

GROUP DIRECTORY

Pass this Directory around and have your Group Members
fill in their names and phone numbers

Name   **Phone**

_____   _____

_____   _____

_____   _____

_____   _____

_____   _____

_____   _____

_____   _____

_____   _____

_____   _____

_____   _____

_____   _____

_____   _____

_____   _____

_____   _____

FOUNDATIONAL TRUTHS

❖ Foundations of the Faith ❖

EDITING AND PRODUCTION TEAM:

James F. Couch, Jr., Lyman Coleman, Sharon Penington, Cathy Tardif,
Christopher Werner, Erika Tiepel, Gregory C. Benoit,
Margaret Harris, Keith Madsen, Scott Lee

NASHVILLE, TENNESSEE

Published by Serendipity House Publishers
Nashville, Tennessee

International Standard Book Number: 1-57494-311-1

ACKNOWLEDGMENTS

Scripture quotations are taken from the Holman Christian Standard Bible,
© Copyright 2000 by Holman Bible Publishers. Used by permission.

Nashville, Tennessee
1-800-525-9563
www.serendipityhouse.com

TABLE OF CONTENTS

CORE VALUES

Community: The purpose of this curriculum is to build community within the body of believers around Jesus Christ.

Group Process: To build community, the curriculum must be designed to take a group through a step-by-step process of sharing your story with one another.

Interactive Bible Study: To share your "story," the approach to Scripture in the curriculum needs to be open-ended and right brain—to "level the playing field" and encourage everyone to share.

Developmental Stages: To provide a healthy program throughout the four stages of the life cycle of a group, the curriculum needs to offer courses on three levels of commitment: (1) Beginner Level—low-level entry, high structure, to level the playing field; (2) Growth Level—deeper Bible study, flexible structure, to encourage group accountability; (3) Discipleship Level—in-depth Bible study, open structure, to move the group into high gear.

Target Audiences: To build community throughout the culture of the church, the curriculum needs to be flexible, adaptable and transferable into the structure of the average church.

Mission: To expand the kingdom of God one person at a time by filling the "empty chair." (We add an extra chair to each group session to remind us of our mission.)

INTRODUCTION

EACH HEALTHY SMALL GROUP WILL MOVE THROUGH VARIOUS STAGES AS IT MATURES.

Multiply Stage: The group begins the multiplication process. Members pray about their involvement in new groups. The "new" groups begin the life cycle again with the Birth Stage.

Birth Stage: This is the time in which group members form relationships and begin to develop community. The group will spend more time in ice-breaker exercises, relational Bible study and covenant building.

Develop Stage: The inductive Bible study deepens while the group members discover and develop gifts and skills. The group explores ways to invite their neighbors and coworkers to group meetings.

Growth Stage: Here the group begins to care for one another as it learns to apply what they learn through Bible study, worship and prayer.

Subgrouping: If you have nine or more people at a meeting, Serendipity recommends you divide into subgroups of 3–6 for the Bible study. Ask one person to be the leader of each subgroup and to follow the directions for the Bible study. After 30 minutes, the Group Leader will call "time" and ask all subgroups to come together for the Caring Time.

Ice-Breaker: Fun, history-giving questions are designed to warm the group and to build understanding about the other group members. You can choose to use all of the Ice-Breaker questions, especially if there is a new group member that will need help in feeling comfortable with the group.

Bible Study: The heart of each meeting is the reading and examination of the Bible. The questions are open, discover questions that lead to further inquiry. Reference notes are provided to give everyone a "level playing field." The emphasis is on understanding what the Bible says and applying the truth to real life. The questions for each session build. There is always at least one "going deeper" question provided. You should always leave time for the last of the "questions for interaction." Should you choose, you can use the optional "going deeper" question to satisfy the desire for the challenging questions in groups that have been together for a while.

Caring Time: All study should point us to actions. Each session ends with prayer and direction in caring for the needs of the group members. You can choose between several questions. You should always pray for the "empty chair." Who do you know that could fill that void in your group?

Sharing Your Story: These sessions are designed for members to share a little of their personal lives each time. Through a number of special techniques, each member is encouraged to move from low risk, less personal sharing to higher risk responses. This helps develop the sense of community and facilitates caregiving.

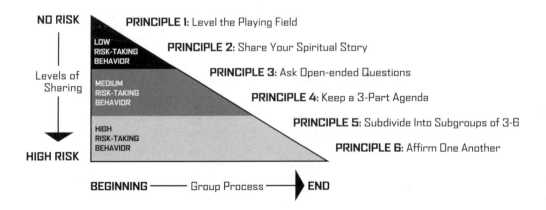

Group Covenant: A group covenant is a "contract" that spells out your expectations and the ground rules for your group. It's very important that your group discuss these issues—preferably as part of the first session.

Ground Rules:

- *Priority:* While you are in the group, you give the group meeting priority.

- *Participation:* Everyone participates and no one dominates.

- *Respect:* Everyone is given the right to their own opinion and all questions are encouraged and respected.

- *Confidentiality:* Anything that is said in the meeting is never repeated outside the meeting.

- *Empty Chair:* The group stays open to new people at every meeting.

- *Support:* Permission is given to call upon each other in time of need—even in the middle of the night.

- *Advice Giving:* Unsolicited advice is not allowed.

- *Mission:* We agree to do everything in our power to start a new group as our mission.

Issues:

- The time and place this group is going to meet is_____.

- Refreshments are _____ responsibility.

- Child care is _____ responsibility.

SESSION 1

THE JOURNEY OF FAITH

SCRIPTURE ACTS 8:26–40

WELCOME

WELCOME TO THIS SMALL GROUP STUDY ON THE FOUNDATIONAL TRUTHS OF CHRISTIANITY. TWO ACTIONS BRING MEN AND WOMEN INTO A RIGHT RELATIONSHIP WITH GOD—CONFESSION AND BELIEF. BEING A FOLLOWER OF JESUS INVOLVES A PUBLIC ACT OF DECLARATION. THROUGHOUT CHRIST'S MINISTRY, HE STRESSED THE IMPORTANCE OF HIS FOLLOWERS SHARING WHAT THEY BELIEVED. THEY SHARED THEIR BELIEFS VERBALLY, AND THEN LIVED OUT WHAT THEY HAD STATED. FROM ITS EARLIEST DAYS, THE CHURCH HAS HAD A NUMBER OF CREEDS OR CONFESSIONS. THE ESSENTIAL BELIEFS WE WILL EXAMINE ARE BASED ON THE APOSTLES' CREED—THE MOST FAMILIAR CONFESSION OF THE CHURCH. WHILE SOME DENOMINATIONS AND AUTONOMOUS CHURCHES ESCHEW ALL CREEDS AS BEING MERE HUMAN DOCUMENTS, MOST NEVERTHELESS HOLD TO THE TRUTHS OF THE APOSTLES' CREED.

The Apostles' Creed is the earliest confession in the Christian Church. It was written at a time when the church was faced with the necessity of countering false teaching that had invaded Christian thinking. They needed a statement that summarized the beliefs of the Christian faith as it had been handed down by the apostles. The Apostles' Creed was written around 150 A.D. and is unique in that it summarizes the basic tenets of the Christian faith, which have withstood the test of time.

We will not cover every part of the creed—only the major themes. In this study, we will examine the six foundations of our faith:

- God the Father
- Jesus Christ
- The Holy Spirit
- The church universal
- The forgiveness of sins
- The life everlasting

Every session has three parts: (1) **Ice-Breaker**—to get to know each other better and introduce the topic, (2) **Bible Study**—to share your own life through a passage of Scripture, and (3) **Caring Time**—to share prayer concerns and pray for one another.

ICE-BREAKER   15 min

CONNECT WITH YOUR GROUP

LEADER

Be sure to read the introductory material in the front of this book prior to the first session. To help your group members get acquainted, have each person introduce him or herself and then take turns answering one or two of the Ice-Breaker questions. If time allows, you may want to discuss all three questions.

Today we will be studying about a man coming back from a long trip who picked up a hitchhiker and was rewarded with eternal benefits. To begin our own "journey" together and get better acquainted, take turns sharing a little about your own history with trips and hitchhikers.

1. When you were a child or teenager, what long trip did you enjoy taking with your family? Where did you go and why did you go

2. When you were returning home from a long trip as a child or teenager, what did you enjoy doing on the ride home?
    • Reading a book.
    • Sleeping in the car.
    • Talking with my siblings.
    • Playing car games.
    • Other _____.

3. When you are on a trip today, what is your policy on picking up hitchhikers or stranded motorists? Have you ever had a good experience doing so?

BIBLE STUDY	30 min

READ SCRIPTURE AND DISCUSS

LEADER

Select a member of the group ahead of time to read aloud the Scripture passage. Then discuss the Questions for Interaction, dividing into subgroups of three to six. Be sure to save time at the end for the Caring Time.

In today's passage, the Holy Spirit leads Philip, a Christian evangelist, to an Ethiopian eunuch who is trying to understand Scripture. Philip helps the eunuch see that Jesus' death and resurrection fulfilled the ancient prophecy of Isaiah 53, and, as a result, the eunuch believes and is baptized. As we look at the basics of the faith, God will also call forth a response from us, as he did from this eunuch. Read Acts 8:26–40, and note how Philip leads the eunuch to faith in Jesus.

Philip and the Ethiopian

[26]An angel of the Lord spoke to Philip: "Get up and go south to the road that goes down from Jerusalem to desert Gaza." [27]So he got up and went. There was an Ethiopian man, a eunuch and high official of Candace, queen of the Ethiopians, who was in charge of her entire treasury. He had come to worship in Jerusalem [28]and was sitting in his chariot on his way home, reading the prophet Isaiah aloud.

[29]The Spirit told Philip, "Go and join that chariot."

[30]When Philip ran up to it, he heard him reading the prophet Isaiah, and said, "Do you understand what you're reading?"

[31]"How can I," he said, "unless someone guides me?" So he invited Philip to come up and sit with him. [32]Now the Scripture passage he was reading was this:

> "He was led like a sheep to the slaughter,
> and as a lamb is silent before its shearer,
> so He does not open His mouth.

[33]
> In His humiliation justice was denied Him.
> Who will describe His generation?
> For His life is taken from the earth."

[34]The eunuch replied to Philip, "I ask you, who is the prophet saying this about—himself or another person?" [35]So Philip proceeded to tell him the good news about Jesus,

beginning from that Scripture.

³⁶As they were traveling down the road, they came to some water. The eunuch said, "Look, there's water! What would keep me from being baptized?" ³⁷And Philip said, "If you believe with all your heart you may." And he replied, "I believe that Jesus Christ is the Son of God." ³⁸Then he ordered the chariot to stop, and both Philip and the eunuch went down into the water, and he baptized him. ³⁹When they came up out of the water, the Spirit of the Lord carried Philip away, and the eunuch did not see him any longer. But he went on his way rejoicing. ⁴⁰Philip appeared in Azotus, and passing through, he was evangelizing all the towns until he came to Caesarea.

Acts 8:26–40

QUESTIONS FOR INTERACTION

LEADER

Refer to the Summary and Study Notes at the end of this session as needed. If 30 minutes is not enough time to answer all of the questions in this section, conclude the Bible Study by answering questions 6 and 7.

1.   If you had been the Ethiopian eunuch and Philip offered you direction while you studied the Bible, how would you have reacted?
  • "Sorry, I don't pick up hitchhikers!"
  • "Do I know you?"
  • "I can figure it out myself, thank you!"
  • "I'm always open to another opinion."
  • "This stuff is totally over my head—I'd be glad for your help!"

2.   Compared to the Ethiopian official, how would you rate your own understanding of Scripture?
  • I've never been as interested in Scripture as he was.
  • I share his interest—and his confusion.
  • I may know a little more than he did, but there is still much I don't understand.
  • While questions remain, I have a pretty good grasp of Scripture and what it says about faith.

3.   What would you say was the most important key to Philip's success in sharing his faith in this story?

4. What passage of Scripture was the eunuch reading? Where can it be found? Why was it a particularly relevant passage for Philip to share what Jesus had done?

5. Why did the eunuch want to be baptized? What could Philip have said that would have made him respond this way?

6. In your spiritual journey, what "Philip" has come alongside you and helped you find direction? What was the most important spiritual truth that this person passed on to you?

7. If a "Philip" could answer your toughest question about faith, what would that question be?
    • Like the Ethiopian's—Who was Jesus and why did he die?
    • Why do so many people suffer?
    • How can I find my role and purpose in life?
    • What is the afterlife like?
    • How can I forgive someone who has hurt me?
    • How can I open myself to the Holy Spirit?
    • Other _____.

GOING DEEPER

If your group has time and/or wants a challenge, go on to these questions.

8. How can a person determine when the Holy Spirit is leading him or her to do something (like talking to a stranger), and when it's just his or her own impulses?

9. Why did God let his Son experience injustice (v. 33)? What does this mean for Jesus' role as Savior?

CARING TIME   15 min

APPLY THE LESSON AND PRAY FOR ONE ANOTHER

LEADER

Take some extra time in this first session to go over the group covenant and ground rules found at the beginning of this book. At the close, pass around your books and have everyone sign the Group Directory.

This very important time is for developing and expressing your concern for each other as group members by praying for one another.

1.   Agree on the group covenant and ground rules found in the introductory pages.

2.   How do you feel about sharing the good news of Jesus with others? What do you need most from the Holy Spirit to help you with taking that risk?

3.   Share any other prayer requests and then close in prayer. Pray specifically for God to bring someone into your life to fill the empty chair.

NEXT WEEK

Today we considered what it was like to begin a spiritual journey by learning the basics of the faith, in the manner of the Ethiopian eunuch. We were reminded that we could all use some help to find our way along the journey of faith. In the coming week, talk with your pastor or a mature Christian about questions you might have regarding your faith. Next week we will get more specific and focus on what the Christian faith teaches about God the Father.

NOTES ON ACTS 8:26 - 40

Summary: Philip was a disciple who was sensitive to the guidance of the Holy Spirit and had a gift for helping others. He knew how to gently and effectively respond to a seeker's questions. In today's Scripture, the Spirit leads him to the chariot of an Ethiopian eunuch, where he answers questions about the prophecy of Christ in Isaiah 53. This provides a good starting place for him to share the "basics" about Jesus, the Christ.

8:26 *An angel of the Lord.* This is a Jewish expression for the Spirit of God (vv. 29,39). *the road.* Two roads, one of which went through a desert area, led from Jerusalem to the old city of Gaza.

8:27 *eunuch.* Eunuchs were commonly employed as royal officials. Although attracted to Judaism, as a eunuch he would never be allowed to fully participate in the temple worship (Deut. 23:1). *Candace.* A dynastic title for the Ethiopian queens.

8:28 *chariot.* While we have visions of light war chariots racing along behind fleet Arabian horses, it is probable that the eunuch was in a slow-moving, ox-drawn cart accompanied by a retinue of servants.

8:34 *who is the prophet saying this about.* The eunuch's question was a common one in Jewish circles. Some thought the prophet was speaking of his own sufferings as one rejected, while others thought he was speaking figuratively of Israel as a nation that suffered at the hands of its oppressors (Isa. 44:1–2). Still another view of the Servant's identity linked him with Cyrus the King of Persia (Isa. 44:28—45:3). The traditional rabbis had not made any connection between the Suffering Servant of Isaiah 53, the kingly Messiah of Isaiah 11 and the glorified Son of Man in Daniel 7:13. Only in Jesus' teachings did these concepts come together (Luke 24:26).

8:35 Philip used this passage as a jumping off point to explain the mission of Jesus and the work of the kingdom. He undoubtedly referred the eunuch to other verses in Isaiah 53, as well as to the other references about the Servant in Isaiah. All of this would have been related to Jesus' ministry, death and resurrection. *Philip proceeded to tell.* Literally, "opened up his mouth." It connotes a solemn pronouncement. *the good news.* This Gospel is not gloom and doom, but a message of joy—God came in Christ to take on and defeat suffering and death.

8:36 *What would keep me from.* This fulfills the prophecy of Isaiah 56:3–8, which anticipates a time when both foreigners and eunuchs would be welcomed into God's household. Luke may have included this particular story to illustrate just that truth. Verse 37 is an addition not found in the earliest manuscripts. A Christian scribe who wished to highlight what was required of a candidate for Christian baptism apparently added it at a later date.

8:39 *carried Philip away.* Whether this was a miraculous act of God (1 Kin. 18:12) or another way of describing a command of the Spirit to Philip (v. 26) is uncertain. *rejoicing.* The joy of the eunuch reflects that of the believers in Jerusalem (2:46) and Samaria (8:8), another evidence of the Spirit.

8:40 *Azotus.* Another city on the coast of the Mediterranean Sea about 20 miles north of Gaza. *Caesarea.* The Roman seat of power in Judea, about 60 miles up the coast from Azotus. Philip evangelized throughout the Jewish communities along the Palestinian coast of the Mediterranean.

SESSION 2

GOD THE FATHER

SCRIPTURE   ACTS 17:16–34

LAST WEEK

IN LAST WEEK'S SESSION, WE CONSIDERED THE STORY OF PHILIP AND THE ETHIOPIAN EUNUCH—
A STORY OF SPIRITUAL BEGINNINGS. WE WERE ENCOURAGED TO SEE HOW GOD WILL PROVIDE
ANSWERS FOR THOSE WHO SEEK TO FIND OUT THE TRUTH ABOUT THEIR FAITH.
THIS WEEK WE WILL SEEK TO LEARN THE TRUTH ABOUT WHAT THE CHRISTIAN
FAITH TEACHES REGARDING GOD THE FATHER.

There are some essential differences between the views of the Hebrew or Jewish people and the way other religions think about God. Judaism claims that there is one God who made everything and everyone. Christianity retains this view. (God reveals himself in three Persons: the Father, Son and Holy Spirit. But they are not three Gods.) A second important distinctive view the Jews have of God is that God is righteous and demands righteous behavior. Thirdly, the Jewish faith teaches that God is not made with human hands (like an idol), nor is God identified with any physical part of creation (like the sun or moon). Rather, God is Spirit and is beyond human comprehension. Christianity holds onto these truths. And in addition, Christianity asserts that because God loves the world, he sent his Son, Jesus Christ, to reveal himself to us and to die for us.

ICE-BREAKER

15 min

CONNECT WITH YOUR GROUP

LEADER

Begin the session with a word of prayer. Have your group members take turns sharing their responses to one, two or all three of the Ice-Breaker questions. Be sure that everyone gets a chance to participate.

Today we will hear of a great debate between Paul and the philosophers of Athens. All of us have probably had our own experiences dealing with the conflict that can surround differing opinions. Take turns sharing a little about your own experiences with heated discussions.

1.   When you were a youth, with whom were you most likely to get into an argument? How did you generally fare in those arguments?

2. As a teenager, where was the place you and your friends most frequently gathered to talk things over?

3. What topic can cause lively debates when your relatives or friends get together now?
   - Politics.
   - Lifestyle issues.
   - Sports.
   - Religion.
   - Other _____ .

BIBLE STUDY   30 min

READ SCRIPTURE AND DISCUSS

LEADER

Select two members of the group ahead of time to read aloud the Scripture passage. Have one member read the part of Luke, the narrator; the other the part of Paul; and have the rest of the group read the part of the philosophers. Then discuss the Questions for Interaction, dividing into subgroups of three to six.

The apostle Paul is well known for his boldness in speaking out. He started by taking his message to the Jewish synagogues, but then went on to the heart of one of history's great philosophical centers—ancient Athens. There he confronted the popular views of his day and told people why the Gospel offered a more complete understanding of who God is and what God expects of us. We also can learn from his answers. Read Acts 17:16–34, and note the reaction of the philosophers.

Paul in Athens

Luke: [16]While Paul was waiting for them in Athens, his spirit was troubled within him when he saw that the city was full of idols. [17]So he reasoned in the synagogue with the Jews and with those who worshiped God, and in the marketplace every day with those who happened to be there. [18]Then also, some of the Epicurean and Stoic philosophers argued with him. Some said,

Philosophers: "What is this pseudo-intellectual trying to say?" … "He seems to be a preacher of foreign deities"

Luke: —because he was telling the good news about Jesus and the resurrection. [19]They took him and brought him to the Areopagus, and said,

Philosophers: "May we learn about this new teaching you're speaking of? [20]For what you say sounds strange to us, and we want to know what these ideas mean."

Luke: [21]Now all the Athenians and the foreigners residing there spent their time on nothing else but telling or hearing something new. [22]Then Paul stood in the middle of the Areopagus and said:

Paul: "Men of Athens! I see that you are extremely religious in every respect. [23]For as I was passing through and observing the objects of your worship, I even found an altar on which was inscribed:

TO AN UNKNOWN GOD

Therefore, what you worship in ignorance, this I proclaim to you. [24]The God who made the world and everything in it—He is Lord of heaven and earth and does not live in shrines made by hands. [25]Neither is He served by human hands, as though He needed anything, since He Himself gives everyone life and breath and all things. [26]From one man He has made every nation of men to live all over the earth and has determined their appointed times and the boundaries of where they live, [27]so that they might seek God, and perhaps they might reach out and find Him, though He is not far from each one of us. [28]For in Him we live and move and exist, as even some of your own poets have said, 'For we are also His offspring.' [29]Being God's offspring, then, we shouldn't think that the divine nature is like gold or silver or stone, an image fashioned by human art and imagination.

    [30]"Therefore, having overlooked the times of ignorance, God now commands all people everywhere to repent, [31]because He has set a day on which He is going to judge the world in righteousness by the Man He has appointed. He has provided proof of this to everyone by raising Him from the dead."

Luke: [32]When they heard about resurrection of the dead, some began to ridicule him. But others said,

Philosophers: "We will hear you about this again."

Luke: ³³So Paul went out from their presence. ³⁴However, some men joined him and believed, among whom were Dionysius the Areopagite, a woman named Damaris, and others with them.

Acts 17:16–34

QUESTIONS FOR INTERACTION

LEADER

Refer to the Summary and Study Notes at the end of this session as needed. If 30 minutes is not enough time to answer all of the questions in this section, conclude the Bible Study by answering questions 6 and 7.

1. Why was Paul so "troubled" by the idols he found in Athens?
   • He was experiencing "culture shock."
   • He realized his work was cut out for him.
   • He knew what kind of immorality was associated with those idols.
   • Other _____.

2. Where have you gone recently and found yourself shocked by your surroundings? How did your reaction compare to Paul's?

3. What do you think convinced these Athenians to give Paul a chance to speak in the Areopagus?

4. Are you more likely to think of God as "unknown" and perhaps unknowable, as some of the Greeks did, or as one who is "not far from each one of us" (v. 27), as Paul taught? What has led you to your position?

5. What do you think was the most effective thing Paul did in Athens?
   • Affirming the philosophers for their religious inclinations.
   • Referring to the poets and thinkers of Greece.
   • Showing the fallacy of worshiping gods made by hands.
   • Boldly proclaiming the resurrection of the dead to those who were skeptical about it.
   • Other _____.

6.   What do you think was the most essential truth about the nature of God that Paul taught in Athens—the truth that people of all ages need to remember, if they remember nothing else?

  • God is the Creator of everything (v. 24).
  • Our shrines, temples and church buildings cannot contain God—he is bigger than them all (v. 25).
  • God is the God of all peoples, not just one nation (v. 26).
  • God reaches out to us, and wants us to reach out to him (v. 27).
  • God is bigger than anything we can conceive (v. 29).
  • God calls for righteous behavior, and repentance when we are not righteous (v. 30).
  • God will one day judge us all (v. 31).
  • God raised Christ from the dead (v. 31).

7.   Where are you right now in terms of this story? Who do you identify with in the story? What do you believe about God?

GOING DEEPER

If your group has time and/or wants a challenge, go on to these questions.

8.   If indeed God does not live in structures made by human hands, why do we spend so much money on church buildings?

9.   In sharing your testimony with someone of another faith, what is the proper balance between acknowledging the insights of that faith (v. 28), and declaring the uniqueness of what Christ has done (v. 31)?

| CARING TIME | 15 min |

APPLY THE LESSON AND PRAY FOR ONE ANOTHER

LEADER

Bring the group back together for the Caring Time. Begin by sharing responses to all three questions. Then share prayer requests and close in a group prayer. Those who don't feel comfortable praying out loud should not feel pressured to do so. As the leader, conclude the prayer time and be sure to pray for the empty chair.

To speak of a church in the true sense is not to speak of a building, but of a group of supportive people of faith. Now is our time to be that for each other, as we share our responses to the following questions and offer our prayer requests.

1.   What was the best thing that happened to you last week? What was the worst?

2.   What "idols" in your life tend to distract you from being fully committed to God? What support do you need from this group in setting these idols aside?

3.   How can this group help you to know God better?

P.S. Add new group members to the Group Directory at the front of this book.

NEXT WEEK

Today we considered who God is and how we can know him better. Paul reminded us, in his debate with the philosophers, that there is one God, he created us and he reaches out to every person, regardless of nationality or background. In the coming week, read Acts 17:24–31 again, and think about how your own view of God compares to Paul's description. Next week we will focus on the One who came to reveal God to us, and reconcile us to him—Jesus Christ.

NOTES ON ACTS 17:16 - 34

Summary: Paul reacted in four different ways to the "culture shock" he experienced in Athens:

(1) His first reaction was one of dismay—verse 16 says he was "troubled."
(2) After his initial shock, Paul turned to a more positive reaction of affirming what was good (v. 22).
(3) Then he spoke to the Athenians in the language of their culture. He referred to their altar "to an unknown god" (v. 23) and to the teachings of their poets (v. 28).
(4) While Paul adapted the form of the message to the culture of Athens, he did not compromise the message itself (1 Cor. 15:12–28).

17:18 *Epicurean and Stoic philosophers.* Epicurus maintained that a tranquil life free from pain, passions and fears was the highest good for humanity. This could be achieved only by detaching oneself from indulgence and the cares of the world. The Epicureans were practical atheists in that they believed the gods had no interest in humanity and were unknowable. The Stoics had a pantheistic idea of god as the World-Soul. People were a spark of the divine; upon death, one's immortal soul would be absorbed into the divine spirit. The ideal life was one of virtue that refused to give in before the pressures of circumstances and of human passions. *this pseudo-intellectual.* Literally, "seed-picker." A derisive term stemming from the actions of a bird that picks up seeds wherever it can find them. To the philosophers, Paul seemed like someone who picked up scraps of ideas here and there and then had the audacity to try to teach others.

17:19 *Areopagus.* Athens was a free city within the Roman Empire so the Areopagus had legal and judicial authority over what went on in the city. It does not appear that Paul himself is on trial (as though he was accused of breaking any laws) as much as his message itself is being evaluated as to its credibility and worth.

17:23 *TO AN UNKNOWN GOD.* Other writers of the time speak of statues and altars in Athens raised to gods "both known and unknown."

17:25 *Neither is He served by human hands.* With this, the philosophers would also agree. Plato had written, "What advantage accrues to the gods from what they get from us?"

17:30 *having overlooked the times of ignorance.* This reflects the Old Testament notion that sins committed in ignorance are less culpable than those done in defiance.

17:32–34 The converts included Dionysius, a member of the Athenian council. Nothing more is said in the New Testament about Athens, so it is unlikely that these believers established a church at the time.

SESSION 3

JESUS CHRIST

SCRIPTURE   MATTHEW 16:13–27

LAST WEEK

Traditional teaching about Jesus Christ posed a problem for the Gnostics, who believed that the material was always inherently evil. They taught that Christ (the divine nature) entered Jesus (the human being) at his baptism, and left the human being at the moment of the Crucifixion. Thus, Christ neither was born a man, nor suffered as a man. Christ (the divine nature) simply used the human body of Jesus for a while. Here then, in the Apostles' Creed, are the basic historical facts concerning Jesus Christ which counter the claims of the Gnostics:

"I believe in Jesus Christ, his only Son, our Lord. He was conceived by the power of the Holy Spirit and born of the virgin Mary. He suffered under Pontius Pilate, was crucified, died, and was buried. He descended into hell. On the third day he rose again. He ascended into heaven, and is seated at the right hand of the Father. He will come again to judge the living and the dead."

ICE-BREAKER   15 min

CONNECT WITH YOUR GROUP

LEADER

Open the session with a word of prayer, and then welcome and introduce any new members. Choose one, two or all three of the Ice-Breaker questions, depending on your group's needs. Remember to stick to the three-part agenda and the time allowed for each segment.

It was obvious that there was something different about Jesus. That difference caused people to ask who he really was. In our Scripture for today, Peter will reflect on some of these perceptions of Jesus' identity. Take turns sharing how different people have perceived your identity at various stages of your life.

1. When you were in high school, how were you viewed by others?
   • As my successful older sibling's younger brother or sister.
   • As my father or mother's child.
   • As "that troublemaker you've heard about."
   • By my achievements.
   • By the potential everyone said I had.
   • As a nobody they didn't really need to know.
   • Other _____.

2. Again, when you were in high school, what did your closest friends know about you that no one else seemed to know?

3. If your closest friend were asked today who you are, what would he or she say (besides the obvious giving of your name)?

BIBLE STUDY   30 min
READ SCRIPTURE AND DISCUSS

LEADER

Select a member of the group ahead of time to read aloud the Scripture passage. Then discuss the Questions for Interaction, dividing into subgroups of three to six. Be sure to save time at the end for the Caring Time.

This is a pivotal passage in Matthew's gospel. Peter's ideas about the Messiah reflect the popular expectations of the Messiah as a political and military hero. These were expectations that Jesus needed to change in order for them to be receptive to a Messiah that brought a spiritual salvation. Read Matthew 16:13–27, and note Jesus' reaction to Peter.

Peter's Confession of Christ

[13]When Jesus came to the region of Caesarea Philippi, He asked His disciples, "Who do people say that the Son of Man is?"

[14]And they said, "Some say John the Baptist; others, Elijah; still others, Jeremiah or one of the prophets."

¹⁵"But you," He asked them, "who do you say that I am?"

¹⁶Simon Peter answered, "You are the Messiah, the Son of the living God!"

¹⁷And Jesus responded, "Blessed are you, Simon son of Jonah, because flesh and blood did not reveal this to you, but My Father in heaven. ¹⁸And I also say to you that you are Peter, and on this rock I will build My church, and the forces of Hades will not overpower it. ¹⁹I will give you the keys of the kingdom of heaven, and whatever you bind on earth will have been bound in heaven, and whatever you loose on earth will have been loosed in heaven."

²⁰And He gave the disciples orders to tell no one that He was the Messiah.

²¹From then on Jesus began to point out to His disciples that He must go to Jerusalem and suffer many things from the elders, chief priests, and scribes, be killed, and be raised the third day. ²²Then Peter took Him aside and began to rebuke Him, "Oh no, Lord! This will never happen to You!"

²³But He turned and told Peter, "Get behind Me, Satan! You are an offense to Me, because you're not thinking about God's concerns, but man's."

²⁴Then Jesus said to His disciples, "If anyone wants to come with Me, he must deny himself, take up his cross, and follow Me. ²⁵For whoever wants to save his life will lose it, but whoever loses his life because of Me will find it. ²⁶What will it benefit a man if he gains the whole world yet loses his life? Or what will a man give in exchange for his life? ²⁷For the Son of Man is going to come with His angels in the glory of His Father, and then He will reward each according to what he has done.

Matthew 16:13–27

QUESTIONS FOR INTERACTION

LEADER

Refer to the Summary and Study Notes at the end of this session as needed. If 30 minutes is not enough time to answer all of the questions in this section, conclude the Bible Study by answering question 8.

1. When have you done something so "solid" that someone could have renamed you "the rock," as Jesus did Simon (vv. 17–18)?

2.   If someone took a poll today, asking the same question that Jesus asked his disciples—"Who do you say that I am?"—which of the following do you think would be the most popular response?
   • A great teacher of morality.
   • A social revolutionary.
   • A mythical figure.
   • The Son of God.
   • The greatest man who ever lived.
   • An influential figure in world history.
   • Other _____.

3.   Why does Jesus switch so quickly from calling Simon "the rock" (v. 18) to calling him "Satan" (v. 23)? What did Peter apparently not understand when he confessed Jesus to be the Christ?

4.   Which of these statements about Christ do you have the hardest time believing?
   • That Jesus is the Son of God (v. 16).
   • That nothing will ever overcome Christ's church (v. 18).
   • That Jesus' death had special significance (v. 21).
   • That Jesus was literally raised from the dead (v. 21).
   • That Jesus is coming again (v. 27).
   • None of this is hard for me to believe.

5.   What does it mean to you to "take up your cross" and follow Christ? What specific acts that you can think of might indicate that a person has truly taken up the cross of Christ?

6.   What would it mean for you to "deny" yourself?

7.   When have you felt like you gave up your "soul" for some temporary thing that wasn't worth it?

8.   What is your answer to the question, "Who is Jesus Christ?" How has your answer changed over time?

GOING DEEPER

If your group has time and/or wants a challenge, go on to these questions.

9. Why was Jesus hesitant to have his disciples reveal at this point that he was the Christ?

10. What does it mean that only those who lose their life for Christ, truly ever find it?

CARING TIME   15 min

APPLY THE LESSON AND PRAY FOR ONE ANOTHER

LEADER

Begin the Caring Time by having group members take turns sharing responses to all three questions. Be sure to save at least the last five minutes for a time of group prayer. Remember to include a prayer for the empty chair when concluding the prayer time.

Denying ourselves means focusing on our brothers and sisters and caring for them. This is a time for doing that. Begin by sharing your responses to the following questions. Then share your prayer requests and close with a time of prayer.

1. Where are you in the journey of following Christ?
   • I am a seeker.
   • I have just begun the journey.
   • I'm returning after getting lost on the wrong path.
   • I've been following Christ for a long time.
   • Other _____.

2. In what ways are you "bound" where this group might help you to become "loosed" (v. 19)?

3. In the coming week, how could you show your appreciation to Jesus for the suffering he went through on your behalf?

NEXT WEEK

Today we focused on the second statement of the Apostles' Creed, and considered who Jesus is and what he did for us. We learned, along with Peter, that Jesus is the promised Messiah, and he came to give us eternal life, not just material wealth and happiness in this life. Next week we will look at the role of the Holy Spirit in our spiritual formation, and how we can open ourselves to his power to help us take up our cross and follow Jesus

NOTES ON MATTHEW 16:13 - 27

Summary: In this passage, Jesus forces his disciples to wrestle with his true identity. The people believed that the Messiah would be a military hero who would lead an army in battle against Rome. Jesus' words about his suffering, death and resurrection are the opposite of this widely held view. It is through Jesus' death that the disciples will discover what kind of Messiah he actually is, and the path of discipleship they are to follow. His disciples are to put to death their own interests for the sake of loyalty to Christ.

16:13 *Caesarea Philippi.* This beautiful city on the slopes of Mount Hermon, 25 miles north of Bethsaida, is also in the region of the headwater of the Jordan River. Although similar in name to the Caesarea on the Mediterranean, this city was rebuilt by Herod the Great's son Phillip, who named it after himself and Tiberius Caesar. It had once been called Balinas, when it was a center for Baal worship, and was later called Paneas because supposedly the god Pan had his birth in a nearby cave. It was an especially pagan area.

16:14 *John / Elijah / Jeremiah.* There was a popular belief that prior to the coming of the Messiah, God would raise up Israel's famous prophets to prepare the way. Many people assumed this was the role played by Jesus (Mal. 4:5).

16:16 *You are the Messiah.* Peter correctly identifies him not as the forerunner of the Christ (the Greek word for "Messiah"), but as the Messiah himself.

16:17 *Simon son of Jonah.* Simon's actual father was John (John 1:42). This figurative term is perhaps meant to identify the disciple with the prophet Jonah who experienced a type of death and resurrection in the great fish. Likewise Peter will suffer, die and rise again, as he identifies with Jesus.

16:18 *Peter.* Peter (a nickname meaning "rock") will become the foundation upon which Christ's church will be built (Eph. 2:20). ***My church.*** The Greek version of the Old

Testament used this word to describe the assembly of Israel. It is only used one other time in the Gospels (18:17).

16:19 *keys of the kingdom of heaven.* This is an allusion to Isaiah 22:15–24 in which God declared that he would give the "key to the house of David" to a new steward who would replace the old one who had been irresponsible.

16:20 Jesus urges them to be silent about what they know. The reason for this is that there were many errant views of who the Messiah would be, and Jesus did not want the people to take some sort of headstrong and mistaken political action against Rome.

16:21 *the elders, chief priests, and scribes.* These three groups made up the Sanhedrin, the official Jewish ruling body.

16:22 *rebuke.* Peter is startled by this teaching that went so much against his notion of who the Messiah was.

16:23 *Get behind Me, Satan!* By urging Jesus to back away from his teaching about suffering, Peter, like Satan, is tempting Jesus with the promise that he can have the whole world without pain (4:8–10). Peter's well-meaning concern betrays an unwillingness to pursue God's agenda rather than his own.

16:24 *come with Me.* This is to take on the role of a disciple, one committed to the teachings of a master. *deny himself.* This does not mean to deny one's own identity or to deny one's principles, but rather to deny control of one's life to self, and to give it to God. *take up his cross.* This symbolized the grisly method of Roman execution, as the only people who bore crosses were prisoners on their way to their death. This would have startled the original hearers, as they thought the Messiah would overthrow Rome. Jesus asserts that to follow him means laying down one's own free choices and putting oneself under the command of Jesus. *follow Me.* This is a call for the disciples to imitate the lifestyle and embrace the values of their teacher.

SESSION 4

THE HOLY SPIRIT

SCRIPTURE   ACTS 1:4–9; 2:1–4,14–17

LAST WEEK

"YOU ARE THE MESSIAH, THE SON OF THE LIVING GOD!" (MATT. 16:16). LAST WEEK WE CONSIDERED THE ONE WHO IS AT THE HEART OF THE CHRISTIAN FAITH—JESUS CHRIST. WE SAW HOW JESUS TAUGHT PETER AND THE DISCIPLES THAT HIS PURPOSE FOR COMING TO EARTH WAS TO SAVE SOULS, NOT TO BE A POLITICAL AND MILITARY HERO. THIS WEEK WE WILL LOOK AT THE THIRD PERSON OF THE TRINITY, THE PART OF GOD WHO IS PERHAPS MOST CONTROVERSIAL AND LEAST UNDERSTOOD—THE HOLY SPIRIT. AS WE DO, WE WILL COME TO A GREATER UNDERSTANDING OF WHO THE SPIRIT IS, AND THE VITAL ROLE THE SPIRIT PLAYS IN THE LIFE OF EVERY CHRISTIAN.

The Spirit is the quiet member of the Trinity. He is mysterious and intangible. Yet throughout the Scriptures, we find the Holy Spirit gently guiding the affairs of the world in general, and the people of God in a special way. The Scriptures reveal several characteristics and roles of the Holy Spirit:

- **Conception and birth of Jesus:** The Holy Spirit was the agent of conception with Mary, the mother of Jesus (Luke 1:30–35).
- **Revelation:** The Holy Spirit is the person of the Trinity who reveals divine truth— particularly in the inspiration and interpretation of Scripture (2 Peter 1:20–21).
- **Conviction of the truth:** The Holy Spirit is the one who is active in bringing the truth to bear upon the hearts of people, convicting people of sin and convincing people of the truth about Jesus Christ (John 16:7–8).
- **Guidance:** The Holy Spirit provides guidance to believers after they have become Christians (John 14:15–18).
- **Power:** The Holy Spirit is the church's power source (Acts 1:8).
- **Gifts for ministry:** The Holy Spirit provides gifts to each believer that each might do ministry to other's on God's behalf (1 Cor. 12).

ICE-BREAKER
15 min

CONNECT WITH YOUR GROUP

LEADER

Begin the session with a word of prayer, and then welcome and introduce new group members. Choose one, two or all three of the Ice-Breaker questions.

Sometimes all you can say is, "You just had to be there!" That is probably how it was when the Holy Spirit came at Pentecost. Before we focus on what the first believers experienced, take turns sharing some of your own experiences, which might prepare us to understand what happened on that day.

1. When have you had an experience in a group that was so amazing and unique that you had a hard time explaining it to people who weren't there?

2. With what other cultures have you had contact as a child or adolescent? Were the relationships between the cultures in your neighborhood relaxed or tense?

3. If you could learn one language that you don't presently know well, what language would you like to learn?

BIBLE STUDY	30 min

READ SCRIPTURE AND DISCUSS

LEADER

Select three members of the group ahead of time to read aloud the Scripture passage. Have one member read the part of Luke, the narrator; another read the part of Jesus; and the third the part of Peter. Ask the rest of the group to read the disciples' part in verse 6. Then discuss the Questions for Interaction, dividing into subgroups of three to six.

The church was "born" just days after the risen Christ's ascension, when the Holy Spirit came upon the believers at Pentecost. Peter quoted from the Old Testament prophet Joel to explain what had happened. Read Acts 1:4–9; 2:1–4,14–17, and note how the Holy Spirit gives boldness to those who were previously in hiding.

The Holy Spirit Comes at Pentecost

Luke: ⁴While He was together with them, He commanded them not to leave Jerusalem, but to wait for the Father's promise.

Jesus: "This," He said, "is what you heard from Me; ⁵for John baptized with water, but you will be baptized with the Holy Spirit not many days from now."

Luke: ⁶So when they had come together, they asked Him,

Disciples: "Lord, at this time are You restoring the kingdom to Israel?"

Jesus: ⁷He said to them, "It is not for you to know times or periods that the Father has set by His own authority. ⁸But you will receive power when the Holy Spirit has come upon you, and you will be My witnesses in Jerusalem, in all Judea and Samaria, and to the ends of the earth."

Luke: ⁹After He had said this, He was taken up as they were watching, and a cloud received Him out of their sight. …

2 When the day of Pentecost had arrived, they were all together in one place. ²Suddenly a sound like that of a violent rushing wind came from heaven, and it filled the whole house where they were staying. ³And tongues, like flames of fire that were divided, appeared to them and rested on each one of them. 4 Then they were all filled with the Holy Spirit and began to speak in different languages, as the Spirit gave them ability for speech. …

¹⁴But Peter stood up with the Eleven, raised his voice, and proclaimed to them:

Peter: "Jewish men and all you residents of Jerusalem, let this be known to you and pay attention to my words. ¹⁵For these people are not drunk, as you suppose, since it's only nine in the morning. ¹⁶On the contrary, this is what was spoken through the prophet Joel:

17   And it will be in the last days, says God,
      that I will pour out My Spirit on all humanity;
      then your sons and your daughters will prophesy,
      your young men will see visions,
      and your old men will dream dreams.

Acts 1:4–9; 2:1–4,14–17

QUESTIONS FOR INTERACTION

LEADER

Refer to the Summary and Study Notes at the end of this session as needed. If 30 minutes is not enough time to answer all of the questions in this section, conclude the Bible Study by answering questions 6 and 7.

1. If you were one of the disciples when Christ was taken up to heaven, how would you have felt about Jesus leaving you?

2. Why was it so important for Jesus to be with the disciples for this forty-day period following his resurrection?

3. Why was it so important for the disciples to wait for the Holy Spirit?

4. What do the images of wind and fire (used here to show the Holy Spirit's presence) suggest to you?
    - Unpredictability—Like wind and fire, I cannot always predict what God will do next through the Spirit.
    - Power—Wind and fire are two of nature's most powerful forces, and remind me of the power of the Spirit.
    - Invisibility—Like the wind and the heat of a fire, I cannot always see the Spirit at work.
    - Change—As wind brings change, the Holy Spirit brings change to the world.
    - Warmth—Fire brings warmth, and the Spirit brings the warmth of love.
    - Other _____.

5. Why do you think God performed this miracle of having people speak in other tongues?

6. In what area of your life do you most need the power of the Holy Spirit?

7. What would you like the Holy Spirit to give you direction or wisdom for right now?

GOING DEEPER

If your group has time and/or wants a challenge, go on to these questions.

8. Why does God not want to reveal to us "times and periods" concerning the coming of his kingdom (1:7)?

9. Where is the church needing to focus more in its mission today: "Jerusalem" (local witness), "Judea and Samaria" (witness to one's own nation), or "to the ends of the earth" (international mission)? Which does your own church do best? Least?

CARING TIME   15 min

APPLY THE LESSON AND PRAY FOR ONE ANOTHER

LEADER

Be sure to save at least 15 minutes for this important time. After sharing responses to all three questions and asking for prayer requests, close in a time of group prayer. Remember to pray for the empty chair.

The Holy Spirit binds us together as a fellowship. One way of expressing that is by supporting and encouraging one another through prayer. Take time now to share your responses to the questions below. Then share your prayer requests and close with a time of prayer.

1. What amazing thing has God done in your life that you would like to thank him for?

2. How can you, individually and as a group, help the mission of your church, both locally and abroad?

3. Pray for the person on your left regarding his or her answer to question 6, and how they most need the Holy Spirit's power and help.

NEXT WEEK

Today we examined the role of the Holy Spirit in our lives and how we can open ourselves to his power. We saw how the disciples became bold in their witness once the Holy Spirit had come upon them. In the coming week, ask the Holy Spirit to guide you each day and give you the strength and boldness to follow God's will for your life. Next week we will focus on the church and how each member of the body of Christ has something to contribute.

NOTES ON ACTS 1:4 – 9; 2:1 – 4,14 – 17

Summary: Acts is the story of how God continued to act even after Jesus returned to be with his Father in heaven. In the first part of our passage, Jesus promises what will happen, and then in the rest of our passages, he fulfills that promise.

1:4 *but to wait.* Jesus was telling them to wait until God empowered and directed them to act. This he was about to do through the sending of the Holy Spirit (ch. 2). While God wants us to act, sometimes it is appropriate to wait until God's power and direction comes (Isa. 40:31). *for the Father's promise.* The Holy Spirit is the promise (Isa. 32:15; Joel 2:28–32; Luke 11:13; 12:12; 24:49; Gal. 3:14). Jesus quotes the words of John the Baptist (Luke 3:16) as a reminder that from the very beginning the expectation was that through him the Spirit of God would be poured out on all people.

1:5 *baptized with the Holy Spirit.* Baptism was associated with cleansing. The metaphor would communicate being flooded with God's Spirit. Thus, Jesus raised the expectations of the disciples regarding what the next step in his agenda for them might be.

1:7 *to know times or periods.* God does not give us a timetable for when history will end. This is similar to what Jesus said in Luke 12:39–40.

1:9 *a cloud received Him out of their sight.* This is not a statement of weather conditions at the time, but a declaration of Jesus' deity.

2:1 *the day of Pentecost.* This was the Feast of Weeks (Ex. 23:16; Lev. 23:15–21; Deut. 16:9–12) held 50 days after Passover. Originally a kind of thanksgiving day for gathered crops, it came to be associated with the commemoration of the giving of the Law at Mount Sinai (Ex. 20:1–17). Pentecost was a celebration which thousands of Jews from all over the empire would attend.

2:2 *a violent rushing wind.* The Greek word for "wind" and "spirit" is the same, hence the symbolism of the Spirit coming like a great wind. Just as humans are powerless to control violent winds like tornadoes and hurricanes, so humans are humbled and helpless before the power of the Holy Spirit. It is a force that we cannot expect to stifle or direct, and yet it brings peace to the soul and glory to God wherever it moves.

2:3 *tongues, like flames of fire.* Fire is often associated with divine appearances (Ex. 3:2; 19:18). John the Baptist said Jesus would baptize his followers with the Holy Spirit and fire (Luke 3:16), symbolizing the cleansing, purifying effect of the Spirit. What is important here is that tongues served as a sign to the crowds of a supernatural event, the point of which was Jesus Christ.

2:4 *filled with the Holy Spirit.* This phrase is found elsewhere (4:8,31; 13:52; Eph. 5:18) indicating a repeatable experience. Here, however, it is clearly associated with the baptism of the Spirit (Acts 1:5), which is an experience new converts enter into upon acceptance of Jesus as the Messiah (11:15-16; 1 Cor. 12:13).

2:15 *are not drunk.* When they saw the ecstatic behavior of the disciples, some observers had accused them of having had too much wine (2:13).

2:17 *your sons and your daughters.* Prophecy was not a gift limited to one sex (21:9; Luke 2:36–38).

SESSION 5

THE CHURCH UNIVERSAL

SCRIPTURE   ACTS 2:42–47

LAST WEEK

IN LAST WEEK'S SESSION, WE FOCUSED ON PENTECOST AND THE COMING OF THE HOLY SPIRIT. WE SAW HOW THE DISCIPLES WERE CHANGED FROM FEARFUL, TIMID MEN IN HIDING INTO BOLD WITNESSES FOR JESUS. WE WERE REMINDED HOW THE SAME HOLY SPIRIT IS AVAILABLE TO US TODAY AND CAN STILL PROVIDE POWER AND STRENGTH TO FOLLOW GOD'S WILL. THIS WEEK WE WILL GAIN SOME UNDERSTANDING ABOUT THE UNIVERSAL CHURCH THAT BEGAN AT PENTECOST, AND HOW EACH BELIEVER HAS A ROLE TO FULFILL IN THAT CHURCH.

The word church comes from a Greek word meaning "to call out." At times it refers to an assembly of people. In the New Testament, the believers are called a "holy temple"— set apart for a special purpose. The Apostles' Creed says, "I believe in ... the holy catholic Church, the communion of saints." The word catholic in the Apostles' Creed means "universal," and refers not to the Roman Catholic Church, but to the "oneness" that all believers have "in Christ." The word saint means one who has been "set apart"; the word communion means fellowship. Thus, the church is described as a fellowship between those who have been set apart by the call of God to be a new family—a very special family that the apostle Paul called "the body of Christ."

ICE-BREAKER   15 min

CONNECT WITH YOUR GROUP

LEADER

Open the session with a word of prayer, and then choose one or two of the Ice-Breaker questions. If you have a new group member, you may want to do all three. Remember to stick closely to the three-part agenda and the time allowed for each segment.

The early disciples shared their possessions freely, making sure that other people's needs were met before their own. Sharing isn't always easy, especially in today's materialistic society. Take turns responding to the following questions about sharing.

1.   When you were in school, which of your possessions were you most likely to share with friends?
   • Clothes, like hats or sweatshirts.   • Cosmetics, jewelry.
   • Records, tapes, CDs.   • Other _____.
   • Bats, ball gloves, athletic equipment.

2.   If you were asked to share what you have with a group right now, what possession would you be most hesitant to share?

3.   How have you recently been sharing your time and talents?

BIBLE STUDY   30 min

READ SCRIPTURE AND DISCUSS

LEADER

Select a member of the group ahead of time to read aloud the Scripture passage. Then discuss the Questions for Interaction, dividing into subgroups of three to six.

After the coming of the Holy Spirit at Pentecost, the church grew and thrived. Many were drawn to the new Christians because of their love and generosity. Read Acts 2:42–47, and note the beautiful fellowship of the early church.

The Fellowship of the Believers

[42]And they devoted themselves to the apostles' teaching, to fellowship, to the breaking of bread, and to prayers.
[43]Then fear came over everyone, and many wonders and signs were being performed through the apostles. [44]Now all the believers were together and had everything in common. [45]So they sold their possessions and property and distributed the proceeds to all, as anyone had a need. [46]And every day they devoted themselves to meeting together in the temple complex, and broke bread from house to house. They ate their food with gladness and simplicity of heart, [47]praising God and having favor with all the people. And every day the Lord added to them those who were being saved.

Acts 2:42–47

QUESTIONS FOR INTERACTION

LEADER

Refer to the Summary and Study Notes at the end of this session as needed. If 30 minutes is not enough time to answer all of the questions in this section, conclude the Bible Study by answering questions 6 and 7.

1. What is the closest you have come to experiencing a fellowship like these believers had together?
    • On a sports team.
    • In my family.
    • In a sorority or a fraternity.
    • In a support group.
    • At a job where I worked.
    • In the cast of a play.
    • With some friends in high school.
    • In a church-related group.
    • Working on a political campaign.
    • I've never come close to having this experience.
    • Other _____.

2. What made the early church so appealing that thousands of people wanted to get in?
    • The food.
    • Their spiritual vitality.
    • The miracles.
    • Great preaching.
    • Their openness to others.
    • Great advertising.
    • The amazing love they had for each other.
    • Their devotion to the apostles' teaching.

3. How do you relate to the early church's practice of having "everything in common" (v. 44)? How do you think you would get along in a community that practiced this early form of socialism?

4. Which of the factors referred to in this passage is the greatest strength of the body of believers with whom you now worship?
   • Joint study.
   • Sharing food and fellowship.
   • Praying together.
   • Caring for each other's needs.
   • Joyful celebration.
   • Other _____.

5. Which of the factors in question 4 is missing most in your present relationship with other believers?

6. If your church began a ministry to meet the greatest need of the people in your community, what need would that be, and what would your church need to "sell" or sacrifice to minister to that need?

7. How does the "harvest" of the church in Acts, where "every day the Lord added to them those who were being saved" (v. 47), compare to that of your own church? What do you see in this passage that might account for any disparity?

GOING DEEPER

If your group has time and/or wants a challenge, go on to these questions.

8. Should the church today be doing "wonders and signs" (v. 43)? What constitutes a "sign"?

9. Is it really possible for a faithful church to have "favor with all the people" (v. 47)? Does faithfulness or necessity sometimes mean irritating certain groups of people?

CARING TIME

15 min

APPLY THE LESSON AND PRAY FOR ONE ANOTHER

LEADER

Conclude the prayer time today by reading Psalm 20:1,4–5: *"May the Lord answer you when you are in distress; may the name of the God of Jacob protect you. ... May he give you the desire of your heart and make all your plans succeed. We will shout for joy when you are victorious and will lift up our banners in the name of our God. May the Lord grant all your requests"* **(NIV).**

In order to have a church like the one in Acts, we must be concerned with each others' needs, which means hearing those needs and praying about them. Take time now to share your responses to the following questions. Then share your prayer requests and close with a time of prayer.

1. How is your relationship with Jesus right now?
    • Close.
    • Distant.
    • Growing apart.
    • Distant.
    • Strained.
    • Other _____.

2. What do you have need of (physically, relationally or spiritually) that you would like this group to be in prayer about?

3. Pray that God would add regularly to the number of your church those who are being saved.

NEXT WEEK

Today we focused on the universal church and looked at the example of the fellowship of the first believers. We were reminded of the essential aspects of what the church should be and do. In the coming week, take some time to evaluate what your role has been in your church and ask the Holy Spirit to help you see if any changes should be made. Next week we will look at one of our greatest blessings as Christians—the forgiveness of our sins.

NOTES ON ACTS 2:42 — 47

Summary: The church that was built through the Holy Spirit in Jerusalem during the infancy of the Christian faith can be seen as a prototype for churches down through the ages. This passage from the second chapter of Acts tells what this church was like, and shows some of the qualities to which the church of today might aspire. The church of this time grew because the Holy Spirit empowered the believers to become a deeply caring community, where God was able to do great deeds. They were also a studying and a worshiping community. The early Christians met every day in the temple courts (v. 46), but not as a refuge from the world. They met to find renewal so they could go into the world with their deeds of love and the message of the Gospel.

2:42 The four components of the church's life here may represent what occurred at their gatherings. *teaching.* The foundation for the church's life was the instruction given by the apostles as the representatives of Jesus. *fellowship.* Literally, "sharing." While this may include the aspect of sharing to meet material needs (v. 45), it most likely means their common participation in the Spirit as they worshiped together (1 Cor. 12). *the breaking of bread.* This refers to the Lord's Supper in which they remembered his death (Luke 22:19) and recognized his presence among them (Luke 24:30–31). *to prayers.* This may refer to set times and forms of prayer as was the practice of the Jews.

2:43–47 The picture of the church is one of continual growth (v. 47) marked by generous sharing (vv. 44–45) and joyful worship and fellowship (vv. 46–47a). The worship at the temple continued as before, since the line dividing Christianity from Judaism had not yet been drawn. Christians simply saw their faith as the natural end of what the Jewish faith had always declared.

2:44 *everything in common.* This was simply an outgrowth of the intense love people had for each other through Jesus Christ. They believed that in Christ each person's need should in some sense become everyone's need. The people decided to take the attitude, "Your need is my need." Then they gave caring to each other that went beyond smiles and well-wishing. It should be noted, however, that while sometimes this practice of sharing possessions worked quite well (4:36–37), at other times people were victimized by greed and deception (5:1–11).

2:47 *And every day the Lord added.* Growth in the church was a natural result of the love, fellowship and commitment to the apostle's teaching that this section describes. Since most churches today, at least those in the most economically privileged sections of western civilization, don't come close to achieving this kind of success in evangelism, we need to consider what caused this growth. In verse 43 we read, "many wonders and signs were being performed through the apostles." This was another way of saying, "miracles." In other words, people's needs were being fulfilled. Just like Jesus' healing ministry created a buzz among the populace (Mark 1:40–45; John 6:1–2), so also did the healing ministry of the early church. We debate back and forth between various denominations and Christian perspectives whether this kind of miraculous healing can be done in the church of today, with our understanding of modern medicine. Rather than debating, we should be focusing on need fulfillment. In the church of this time, medicine was not nearly as advanced as it is today, and so this healing ministry was filling a desperate need that the people had. What similar needs do people have today that the church can address? A church that wants to follow the example of the church in Acts needs to ask that question and seek God's guidance on ways to respond to those needs.

SESSION 6

THE FORGIVENESS OF SINS

SCRIPTURE   JOHN 8:2–11

LAST WEEK

"AND THEY DEVOTED THEMSELVES TO THE APOSTLES' TEACHING, TO FELLOWSHIP, TO THE BREAKING OF BREAD, AND TO PRAYERS" (ACTS 2:42). LAST WEEK WE LOOKED AT THE UNIVERSAL CHURCH AND THE EXAMPLE OF THE FIRST BELIEVERS AS THEY WERE EMPOWERED BY THE HOLY SPIRIT TO REACH OTHERS FOR CHRIST. ONE THING A CHURCH SHOULD CERTAINLY DO IS CONVEY THE FORGIVENESS OF GOD THAT JESUS CHRIST CAME TO BRING. IT IS THAT FORGIVENESS WE WILL STUDY THIS WEEK.

Sin refers to the nature that is bent, twisted and slightly off course. This nature leads to acts of sin that fall short of the mark, and to deliberate disobedience. These acts of sin bring about consequences that include alienation from God, restlessness and, finally, destruction and death. The good news (Gospel) of Jesus Christ is that God made atonement for sin. In the Old Testament, atonement meant "to cover" with the sacrifice of an innocent animal. In the New Testament, the word for atonement of sin took on a whole new meaning in the person and work of Jesus Christ: "Look, the Lamb of God, who takes away the sin of the world" (John 1:29). Jesus Christ has made a complete payment for our sin, and we do not have to pay for our sin anymore.

ICE-BREAKER

15 min

CONNECT WITH YOUR GROUP

LEADER

Begin the session with a word of prayer, asking God for his blessing and presence. Choose one, two or all three Ice-Breaker questions, depending on your group's needs.

Most of us have memories of getting caught doing something wrong as a child and having to stand before an adult, trembling at the prospect of what our punishment might be. The adulterous woman in today's Scripture passage had much to tremble about—she was facing death as a punishment. Take turns sharing those times you got in trouble, or had to judge someone else who was in trouble.

1. When do you remember being caught "red-handed" doing something as a child or adolescent that you weren't supposed to do? How did your parents handle the situation?

2. When you got into trouble as a child, who was most likely to take your defense? Who was most likely to "take the stand" against you?

3. When were you last asked to stand in judgment on someone?
   • When I had jury duty.
   • When I was on a search or personnel committee.
   • When two of my kids blamed something on each other.
   • Other _____.

How did it feel being in this position?

BIBLE STUDY   30 min
READ SCRIPTURE AND DISCUSS

LEADER

Select three members of the group ahead of time to read aloud the Scripture passage. Have one member read the part of John; another the part of Jesus; and the third person the part of the adulterous woman. Ask the whole group to read the part of the Pharisess. Then discuss the Questions for Interaction, dividing into subgroups of three to six.

The following story, whose status in the earliest manuscripts of John is uncertain, is nevertheless one of the best-known and loved stories of God's forgiveness. Through this story we are clearly called to show the kind of forgiveness to others that we want God to show to us. Read John 8:2–11, and note what Jesus tells the woman to do.

Jesus Forgives the Woman Caught in Adultery

John: [2]At dawn He went to the temple complex again, and all the people were coming to Him. He sat down and began to teach them. [3]Then the scribes and the Pharisees brought a woman caught in adultery, making her stand in the center.

Pharisees: ⁴"Teacher," they said to Him, "this woman was caught in the act of committing adultery. ⁵In the law Moses commanded us to stone such women. So what do You say?"

John: ⁶They asked this to trap Him, in order that they might have evidence to accuse Him. Jesus stooped down and started writing on the ground with His finger. ⁷When they persisted in questioning Him, He stood up and said to them,

Jesus: "The one without sin among you should be the first to throw a stone at her."

John: ⁸Then He stooped down again and continued writing on the ground. ⁹When they heard this, they left one by one, starting with the older men. Only He was left, with the woman in the center. ¹⁰When Jesus stood up, He said to her,

Jesus: "Woman, where are they? Has no one condemned you?"

Woman: ¹¹"No one, Lord," she answered.

Jesus: "Neither do I condemn you," said Jesus. "Go, and from now on do not sin any more."

                                                            John 8:2–11

QUESTIONS FOR INTERACTION

LEADER

Refer to the Summary and Study Notes at the end of this session as needed. If 30 minutes is not enough time to answer all of the questions in this section, conclude the Bible Study by answering questions 6 and 7.

1.   What shocks you the most about this story?
     • That the man wasn't hauled before Jesus as well.
     • That they really would consider executing a woman for such an act.
     • That religious people would use this woman as a pawn to get at Jesus.
     • That the accusers could be silenced so easily.
     • Other _____.

2. What is the trap the Pharisees are setting for Jesus? What would it have done to his credibility as a teacher if he would have spoken against what was in the Law of Moses? What would it have done to his status as a compassionate teacher of the people if he had called for her to be stoned?

3. What do you think Jesus was writing on the ground with his finger (see note on v. 6)? Why does he not answer them at first?

4. Who does Jesus call upon to cast the first stone at this woman? Why does he establish this as the criteria?

5. Why do you think that the older Pharisees left first? What does this say about the experience of getting older?

6. When do you remember last receiving a merciful response to something you had done wrong? How did this mercy affect your resolve to not repeat the act?

7. Had Jesus said to you, "Neither do I condemn you ... Go, and from now on do not sin any more," how would you have responded?
    • "Easier said than done."
    • "I'll try."
    • "Thank you, Lord."
    • Other _____.

GOING DEEPER

If your group has time and/or wants a challenge, go on to these questions.

8. What does this story say about the idea that what is needed today to discourage wrong behavior is stricter laws and more stringent punishments? What are the relative roles of punishment and mercy in changing people's behavior?

9. What kind of help does a person need in order to leave behind a life of sin?

CARING TIME

15 min

APPLY THE LESSON AND PRAY FOR ONE ANOTHER

LEADER

Following the Caring Time, discuss with your group how they would like to celebrate the last session next week. Also, discuss the possibility of splitting into two groups or continuing together with another study.

All of us need forgiveness at some time or another. Gather around each other now in this Caring Time and give each other support and encouragement. Take turns sharing your responses to the following questions. Then share your prayer requests and close with a time of prayer.

1. Make a list of the people who have been merciful to you in your life (responses to question 6 will give you a good start). Take time to thank God for these people.

2. If you were in a group to whom Jesus said, "The one without sin among you should be the first to throw a stone at her," what sin of your own would have come to mind? Take time to pray for forgiveness for these sins and strength to deal with them in the future.

3. How do you need God's help in forgiving someone who has hurt you?

NEXT WEEK

Today we focused on the great blessing of God's forgiveness of our sins. We looked at what it meant for the woman taken in adultery, and what it means for us. In the coming week, write your sins down on a piece of paper, and ask God to forgive you for each one, and then destroy the paper, knowing that you are forgiven. Ask the Holy Spirit to help you to "not sin any more." Next week we will conclude our study on the foundational truths of Christianity by considering what our faith teaches about everlasting life.

NOTES ON JOHN 8:2 - 11

Summary: Jesus healed many people physically, but, more importantly, he healed people spiritually through forgiveness. The Law of Moses had called upon those who committed adultery to be stoned. This penalty was rarely carried out, but it was there nonetheless. The woman brought before Jesus was apparently guilty of this sin—caught in the very act. The words that Jesus said to save her, words that have been said many times since to discourage judgmental behavior—"The one without sin among you should be the first to throw a stone at her" (v. 7). As he was setting her free he made one more important pronouncement—"Go, and from now on do not sin any more" (v. 11). God's forgiveness is always meant to lead us to repentance and a moral turn around.

8:3 *scribes and the Pharisees.* The teachers of the law, or scribes, are not mentioned elsewhere in John but play a prominent part in the other Gospels. They were the ordained teachers, serving as the representatives of Moses to the people in interpreting the Law. They were taught as rabbis and acted as lawyers in legal cases. ***a woman caught in adultery.*** Since this sin cannot be committed alone, why was only one offender brought before the temple courts? The teachers of the law and the Pharisees had staged this to trap Jesus (v. 6).

8:5 *Moses commanded us to stone such women.* This was only partially true. Leviticus 20:10 and Deuteronomy 22:22 prescribe that both parties shall be put to death. Since it was said that the woman was caught in the act, the man was also there and should have been brought in as well. The Jews, under Roman law, had no authority to carry out such sentences. In Israel's past, this penalty was rarely carried out because capital offenses required two or three witnesses. The normal result of adultery (on the part of a woman) was divorce. Women could not divorce their husbands for any reason.

8:6 *They asked this to trap Him.* See also Matthew 19:3 and 22:15 for other situations where Jesus' enemies attempted to find some reason for making a charge against him. In this case, if he allowed stoning he would be in violation of Roman law and would be found to be stricter than even the Pharisees in his application of the Law. If he tried to release her, he could be faulted for ignoring the Law of Moses. ***started writing on the ground with His finger.*** It is uncertain what Jesus wrote. However, speculation centers on the possibility he was writing the other commandments, which would remind onlookers of commandments they may have broken.

8:7 *The one without sin among you.* Jesus affirms the validity of the Law, but forces the initiative back on the accusers. Perhaps some of them had in the back of their memory a time when they "sowed some wild oats." This statement does not imply that sinless people can only try judicial cases. It is, however, a rebuke to the base motives of these leaders who would self-righteously forget their own sins while using this woman to **implicate Jesus.**

8:9 *starting with the older men.* The older ones may have had the wisdom of experience to know their own fallibility. The younger ones may not have been old enough to have had their eyes fully open to see themselves as they were.

8:11 *Neither do I condemn you.* This story illustrates the truth of 3:17. The woman had come face-to-face with condemnation, shame and death, but was pardoned by the one to whom all judgment has been given (5:22). *Go, and from now on do not sin any more.* The compassion and mercy of Jesus is related to his call to people to live in obedience to the will of his Father. Paul, likewise, flatly rejects the idea that people can claim God's mercy while actively pursuing a lifestyle that is in opposition to his will (Rom. 6:1–2,15).

LIFE EVERLASTING

SCRIPTURE   1 CORINTHIANS 15:12-22,51-58

LAST WEEK

THE INCREDIBLE BLESSING OF GOD'S FORGIVENESS OF OUR SINS WAS OUR FOCUS IN LAST WEEK'S SESSION. WE SAW HOW JESUS FORGAVE THE WOMAN CAUGHT IN ADULTERY, AND WE WERE REMINDED HOW WE NEED TO HAVE COMPASSION ON OTHERS AND FORGIVE THOSE WHO WRONG US. IN THIS FINAL SESSION, WE WILL CONSIDER WHAT WE CAN LOOK FORWARD TO BECAUSE OF THE FORGIVENESS THAT COMES THROUGH JESUS CHRIST—LIFE EVERLASTING.

The final statement in the Apostles' Creed that we will consider deals with the resurrection of those who believe in Jesus Christ. *"I believe in ... the resurrection of the body, and the life everlasting."*

The resurrection of Jesus Christ from the dead is the cornerstone of the Christian faith. It transformed the early Christians from a defeated, hopeless band of followers into a force of men and women who boldly proclaimed the words of Jesus (because they had seen him after he was raised from the dead). Against the skeptics who questioned Jesus' bodily resurrection, the apostle Paul reasserted the bodily resurrection of Jesus Christ as proof that believers will also conquer death (1 Cor. 15). The resurrection of Jesus Christ proved that they could believe everything he taught them, and that they could expect to live forever. Paul speaks very plainly about this: "Now if we died with Christ, we believe that we will also live with Him" (Rom. 6:8).

ICE-BREAKER   15 min
CONNECT WITH YOUR GROUP

LEADER

Begin this final session with a word of prayer and thanksgiving for this time together. Be sure to affirm each group member for the blessings and contributions that he or she made to the group.

In order to instruct the people of Corinth, as well as his other churches, Paul passed on the stories of Christ that he had learned himself. We also are formed by the stories passed along to us. Take turns sharing some stories that have been important to you.

1. What stories do you remember your parents and/or grandparents passing on to you about your family history? How do you feel about having such "roots"?

2. Who first told you the very basic story of what the Gospel was all about? What do you remember about the story?

3. What story about your life would you like to pass on to future generations in your family?

BIBLE STUDY	30 min

READ SCRIPTURE AND DISCUSS

LEADER

Select a member of the group ahead of time to read aloud the Scripture passage. Then discuss the Questions for Interaction, dividing into subgroups of three to six. Be sure to save some extra time at the end for the Caring Time.

Sometimes we think that skepticism about the resurrection of the dead is a modern phenomenon. But whenever we are tempted to be skeptical we should read the following passage. Here Paul confronts such skepticism with strong words of the centrality of resurrection to the Christian faith. Read 1 Corinthians 15:12–22,51–58, and note the great hope that we have as Christians.

The Resurrection of the Dead

[12]Now if Christ is preached as raised from the dead, how can some of you say, "There is no resurrection of the dead"? [13]But if there is no resurrection of the dead, then Christ has not been raised; [14]and if Christ has not been raised, then our preaching is without foundation, and so is your faith. [15]In addition, we are found to be false witnesses about God, because we have testified about God that He raised up Christ—whom He did not raise up if in fact the dead are not raised. [16]For if the dead are not raised, Christ has not been raised. [17]And if Christ has not been raised, your faith is worthless; you are still in your sins. [18]Therefore those who have fallen asleep in Christ have also perished. [19]If we have placed our hope in Christ for this life only, we should be pitied more than anyone.

[20]But now Christ has been raised from the dead, the firstfruits of those who have fallen

asleep. [21]For since death came through a man, the resurrection of the dead also comes through a man. [22]For just as in Adam all die, so also in Christ all will be made alive. ...

[51]Listen! I am telling you a mystery:
    We will not all fall asleep, but we will all be changed,
[52]   in a moment, in the twinkling of an eye, at the last trumpet.
    For the trumpet will sound, and the dead will be raised incorruptible,
    and we will be changed.
[53]   Because this corruptible must be clothed with incorruptibility,
    and this mortal must be clothed with immortality.
[54]   Now when this corruptible is clothed with incorruptibility,
    and this mortal is clothed with immortality,
    then the saying that is written will take place:
    "Death has been swallowed up in victory.
[55]   O Death, where is your victory?
    O Death, where is your sting?"
[56]   Now the sting of death is sin, and the power of sin is the law.
[57]   But thanks be to God, who gives us the victory
    through our Lord Jesus Christ!
[58]Therefore, my dear brothers, be steadfast, immovable, always excelling in the Lord's work, knowing that your labor in the Lord is not in vain.

1 Corinthians 15:12–22,51–58

QUESTIONS FOR INTERACTION

LEADER

Refer to the Summary and Study Notes at the end of this session as needed. If 30 minutes is not enough time to answer all of the questions in this section, conclude the Bible Study by answering question 7.

1. What was your first experience with death? How did you react? Who or what helped you the most?

2. What false teaching were some people in the Corinthian church believing (v. 12)? Why does this kind of cynicism keep showing up, even in the church?

3. According to Paul, in what way does all of the Christian faith rest upon the reality of resurrection from the dead? Why does he say that if it is not true, Christians are to be pitied even more than others (see notes on vv. 13–19)?

4. What is the "mystery" that Paul seeks to reveal (v. 51)? In what way is death still somewhat of a mystery even after what Paul writes?

5. How does verse 58 encourage and motivate you?

6. Considering what Paul says here, how would you explain the importance of the Resurrection to a non-Christian?

7. When have you had to confront your own mortality in more than merely an intellectual way? Was it because of a serious health problem, the death of a loved one or a community tragedy? Did this make you feel differently about your faith in the resurrection of the dead? In what way?

GOING DEEPER

If your group has time and/or wants a challenge, go on to this question.

8. What does Paul mean by "the sting of death is sin" (v. 56)? How does the presence of sin make the reality of death tragic and painful?

CARING TIME   15 min

APPLY THE LESSON AND PRAY FOR ONE ANOTHER

LEADER

Conclude this final Caring Time by praying for each group member and asking for God's blessing in any plans to start a new group or continue to study together.

Gather around each other now in this final time of sharing and prayer, being confident that God will give each of you the strength, wisdom and grace to understand your faith and pass it along to others.

1. How has this group been a blessing in your life?

2. What are some specific areas in which you have grown in this course?
   • Understanding the foundational truths of the Christian faith.
   • Deepening my commitment to Christ.
   • Developing a greater appreciation for God.
   • Developing a greater appreciation for Jesus.
   • Developing a greater appreciation for the Holy Spirit.
   • Developing a greater appreciation for the church.
   • Gaining a fresh start thanks to the forgiveness of sins.
   • Being renewed in the hope of everlasting life.
   • Other _____.

3. How would you like the group to continue praying for you in the weeks to come?

NOTES ON 1 CORINTHIANS 15:12 – 22, 51 – 58

Summary: In today's passage, Paul confronts the theological issue of resurrection from the dead. Apparently, some Corinthians were denying that in the future believers will be raised from the dead. It's possible that no one had instructed them in this matter. (The Thessalonians, for example, did not know about the resurrection of the dead, as Paul says in 1 Thess. 4:13–18.) However, the Corinthians might have resisted this concept, since it ran counter to the Gnostic idea that death released the spirit to return to God, and the useless body (in the Gnostic view) fell away like a discarded husk. Or, like Hymenaeus and Philetus, they might have "spiritualized" the resurrection, saying that it has already taken place (2 Tim. 2:17–18). Paul begins this chapter by pointing to something the Corinthians believed: that Christ rose from the dead. Christ's resurrection is the key to Paul's argument that believers will also be resurrected.

15:12 *Now.* Having established the fact of Christ's resurrection (15:3–8), Paul now pushes the argument forward: Jesus' resurrection is a clear proof that there is such a thing as resurrection. ***how can some of you say.*** Now Paul pinpoints directly the false teaching against which he is contending.

15:13–15 In the next if/then argument, Paul shows that if resurrection is impossible, then: (a) Christ could not have been raised, (b) Paul's own preaching is without value, (c) their faith is meaningless, and (d) they are lying about God.

15:14 *our preaching / your faith.* The Corinthians owe their very existence as a church to these two things: Paul's preaching and their response of faith. Central to both the preaching and their faith is the resurrection of Christ. And since the church does indeed exist, this is another proof of Christ's resurrection.

15:16 *if the dead are not raised.* This is the first of three times in this section (vv. 12–34) that Paul uses this phrase that summarizes the implications of their errant view about the resurrection of the body. If the dead are not raised, then: (a) Christ could not have been resurrected (and they believe that he was), (b) there would be no point in baptizing people for the dead (as they were apparently doing—v. 29), and (c) believers might as well "live it up," since they had no future (v. 32).

15:17–19 Relentlessly, Paul points out to his readers the implications of no resurrection: (a) they are still lost and dead in sin, (b) those who have died are lost, (c) their "hope" is groundless, and (d) they are pitiable people. Without the resurrection, Christianity crumbles.

15:20 *But now Christ has been raised.* Having sketched the horror of no resurrection, Paul relieves the gloom and shifts to this positive affirmation. This is the essential declaration, without which there is no Christianity. ***firstfruits.*** The early developing grains or fruits that demonstrate that the full harvest is not far behind. Similarly, the fact that Christ was raised from the dead is clear proof that the future resurrection of believers is assured.

15:21–22 From the metaphor of the firstfruits, Paul moves to the analogy of Christ and Adam. It is through Adam that all died. It is through Christ that death is undone. Paul will treat this metaphor in more detail in 15:45–49.

15:22 *Adam.* Adam sinned, and so death entered into the world (Gen. 2:17; 3:6); and thus all people since that time experience death (Rom. 5:12–21). ***all will be made alive.*** Though the wording has been made parallel to the previous clause ("all die"), the idea is that all who are in Christ will rise, as Paul says explicitly in 1 Thessalonians 4:16.

15:51 *mystery.* A truth about the end times, once hidden but now revealed. We. Paul expected to be alive at the Second Coming. *not all fall asleep.* Some Christians will be alive at the Second Coming. *all be changed.* Both the living and the dead will be changed.

15:52 *in a moment.* This change will occur instantaneously. *the trumpet will sound.* The sounding of the trumpet was used to rally an army for action. This image is used to describe God's calling his people together (1 Thess. 4:16). *the dead will be raised.* Those who are in the grave at the Second Coming will be transformed, as will the living.

15:54 *the saying that is written will take place.* Paul cites two texts from the Old Testament—here (the quote is from Isa. 25:8) and in verse 55—which have yet to be fulfilled.

15:56 *the power of sin is the law.* By this Paul means that the Law has the unfortunate result of arousing sin within people. As he shows from his own example in Romans 7, the Law's command not to covet did not deliver him from covetousness but actually stirred him up to feel it all the more.

15:57 *victory.* In great joy, Paul exults in the fact that sin and the Law (that by which sin is made known) do not have the last word. Christ's death was a victory over sin and death.

15:58 *be steadfast.* His letter is at an end; his chastening is finished, and so it is appropriate that he challenge them to allow this same Christ who has won victories for them to win victories through them. *your labor in the Lord is not in vain.* Because the Resurrection is real, the future is secure and magnificent.

PERSONAL NOTES

PERSONAL NOTES

PERSONAL NOTES

PERSONAL NOTES

PERSONAL NOTES

PERSONAL NOTES